STEM Projects in MINECRAFT™

The Unofficial Guide to Building Castles in MINECRAFT™

JILL KEPPELER AND SAM KEPPELER

PowerKiDS press
New York

Published in 2019 by The Rosen Publishing Group, Inc.
29 East 21st Street, New York, NY 10010

Copyright © 2019 by The Rosen Publishing Group, Inc.

All rights reserved. No part of this book may be reproduced in any form without permission in writing from the publisher, except by a reviewer.

First Edition

Editor: Greg Roza
Book Design: Rachel Rising
Illustrator: Matías Lapegüe

Photo Credits: Cover, pp. 1, 3, 4, 6, 8, 10, 12, 14, 16, 18, 20, 22, 23, 24 (background) Evgeniy Dzyuba/Shutterstock.com; pp. 6, 8, 10, 12, 14, 18 (insert) Levent Konuk/Shutterstock.com; p. 7 canadastock/Shutterstock.com; p. 11 Matt Trommer/Shutterstock.com; p. 22 Ljupco Smokovski/Shutterstock.com.

Cataloging-in-Publication Data

Names: Keppeler, Jill. | Keppeler, Sam.
Title: The unofficial guide to building castles in Minecraft / Jill Keppeler and Sam Keppeler.
Description: New York : PowerKids Press, 2019. | Series: STEM projects in Minecraft | Includes index.
Identifiers: LCCN ISBN 9781508169260 (pbk.) | ISBN 9781508169253 (library bound) | ISBN 9781508169284 (6 pack)
Subjects: LCSH: Minecraft (Game)–Juvenile literature. | Minecraft (Video game)–Handbooks, manuals, etc.–Juvenile literature.
Classification: LCC GV1469.M55 K47 2019 | DDC 794.8–dc23

Manufactured in the United States of America

CPSIA Compliance Information: Batch #CS18PK: For Further Information contact Rosen Publishing, New York, New York at 1-800-237-9932

Contents

Full of Possibility 4
Castles in Real Life 6
Minecraft Blocks 8
Choosing a Site 10
Kinds of Castles 12
Walls and Halls and Towers 14
Inside the Walls 16
Moats and Drawbridges 18
What Will You Build? 20
Making Mods 22
Glossary 23
Index 24
Websites 24

Full of Possibility

Imagine that you're standing on a mountaintop. Spread out before you is a wide, wonderful world full of possibilities. You can see hills and forests and rivers. You can explore and build anything you want to. All you need is a plan!

Minecraft is a sandbox game, which means players can roam the game world at will, building structures and changing the land. You can create some amazing things in the game and you can learn a lot about how building and engineering work. Creating huge, fancy structures such as castles can be easy if you understand the principles.

> Even *Minecraft*'s many monsters will have a hard time getting into a sturdy castle tower like this one.

Materials:

LAVA

GRASS

STONE

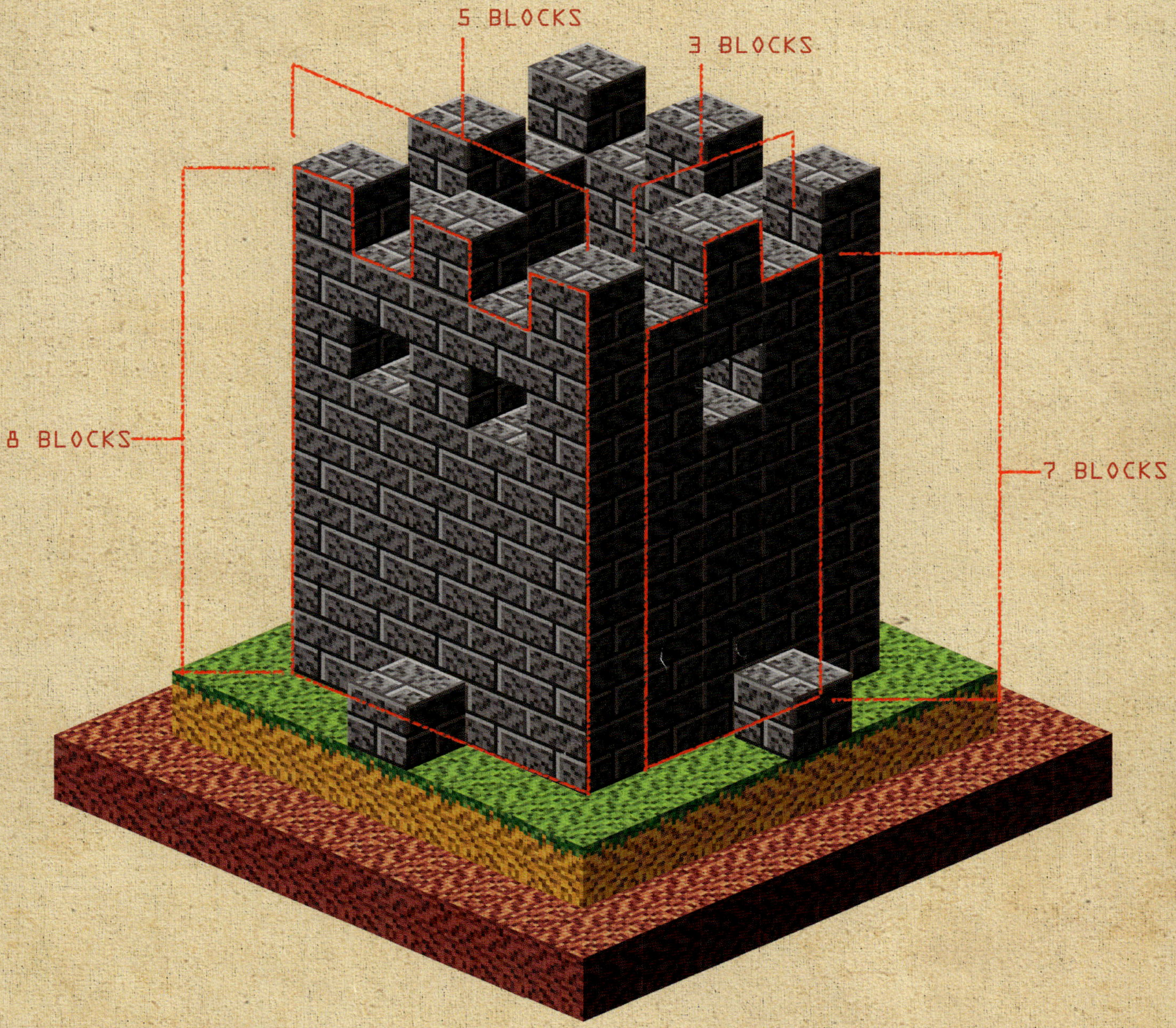

5 BLOCKS

3 BLOCKS

8 BLOCKS

7 BLOCKS

5

Castles in Real Life

Castles became common in Europe during **medieval** times. These strongholds protected kings and lords and their people and gave them a safe place to live. They were surrounded by **fortified** walls and had strong buildings and many **defenses**. What we think of as castles today were first built by the **Normans** in the late ninth and 10th centuries.

People in other parts of the world, including Japan and India, have also used castles throughout history, but this book will look at **designs** for European castles. Since castles are meant to protect people, they make a great way to protect your *Minecraft* characters and belongings!

MINECRAFT MANIA

One of the most famous castles of all is Neuschwanstein Castle in Bavaria. It's beautiful, but it was never finished. Still, more than 1 million people visit it each year.

Can you imagine building Neuschwanstein Castle in *Minecraft*? That would take a lot of work! People have done it, however. Could you?

Minecraft Blocks

Almost everything in *Minecraft* is made of blocks. There are blocks of grass, dirt, and different kinds of stone making up the ground. Blocks of wood and leaves make up trees. You can mine blocks of ore and other **resources** underground. There are even blocks of water and lava!

These blocks don't follow real-world **physics**, however. Most aren't affected by gravity, which means you can stack them in strange shapes and they won't fall. This makes it easier to build things. A few blocks, such as gravel and sand, are affected by gravity. They will fall if there's nothing under them.

MINECRAFT MANIA

You can play *Minecraft* in several different **modes**. If you play in Creative mode, you'll have all the blocks you want without gathering them. And you can fly!

In real castles, arches like this one were sometimes used because they could support a lot of weight. The weight of the stones is carried by the supports, not the bricks in the middle. In *Minecraft*, however, you don't have to worry about this!

Choosing a Site

You'll need a lot of open space to build a castle. You may have to look for a plains **biome** for empty, flat space, or you may have to chop down a lot of trees and level (or build up) the ground. You can use *Minecraft* TNT, an **explosive**, to help clear hills quickly. Just make sure to stand back if you're playing in Survival mode!

You may want to keep the land as it is, though. Many historical castles were built at the sides of mountains or hills. Sometimes the main building of a castle was built at the top of a hill.

MINECRAFT MANIA

If you want your castle to have its own people like a medieval castle would, you can build it near or around a nonplayer character (NPC) village. You can protect the villagers!

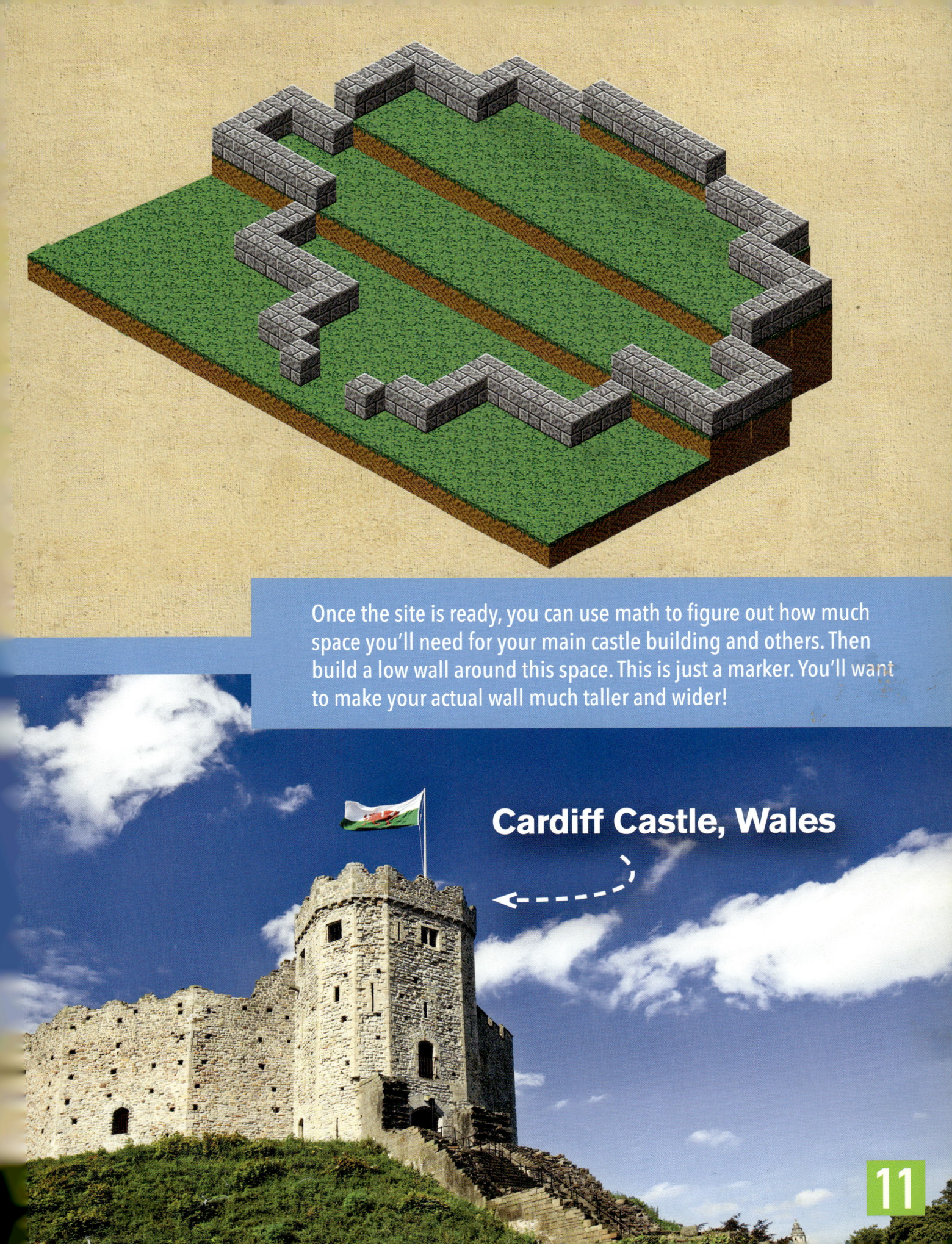

Once the site is ready, you can use math to figure out how much space you'll need for your main castle building and others. Then build a low wall around this space. This is just a marker. You'll want to make your actual wall much taller and wider!

Cardiff Castle, Wales

Kinds of Castles

There were three main types of castles during medieval times. The earliest (and simplest) was the motte and bailey, which was generally made out of wood. A wooden fort stood on top of a hill (the motte), other buildings stood at the hill's base (in the bailey), and a wall surrounded both.

Stone keep castles followed motte-and-bailey castles. These had tall walls, towers, and a sturdy rectangular keep, or main building, that was made of stone. They were followed by **concentric** castles, which had multiple layers of walls. These are the strongest castles.

MINECRAFT MANIA

You might want to use stone for the same reason medieval people did. It's much stronger than wood and it won't burn. (Although medieval people didn't have to worry about creepers blowing up their castles!)

In *Minecraft*, most kinds of stone have a higher blast resistance than wood. This means that if there's an explosion caused by TNT or a creeper, a stone building will take less damage than a wooden one.

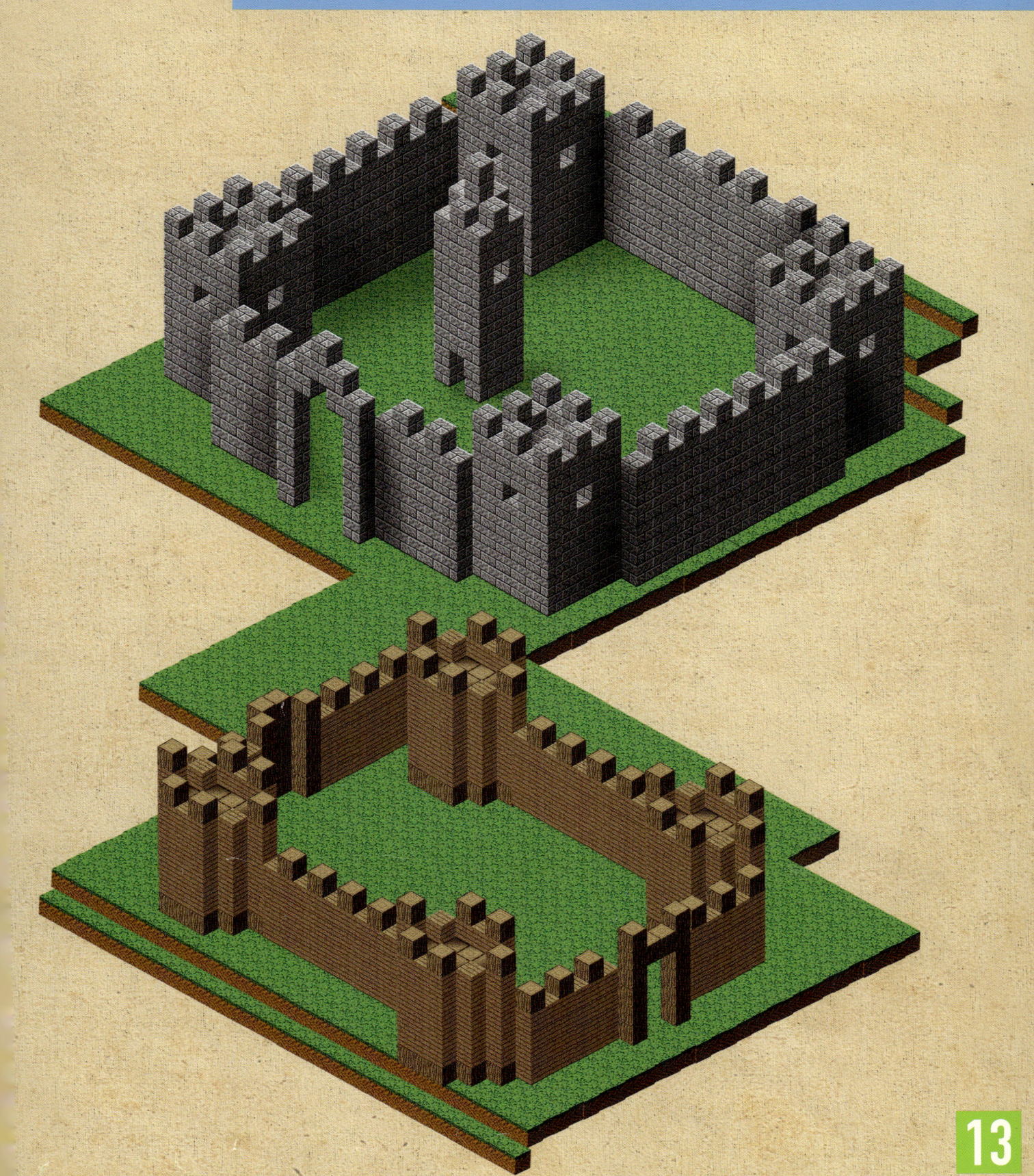

Walls and Halls and Towers

Once you have a site and you've decided what kind of castle you want to build, it's time to start raising the walls. Castle walls can be very thick. Sometimes guards would patrol the tops of these walls and keep an eye out for danger. If you're playing in Survival mode, you'll need some type of **scaffolding** to keep you from falling as you build. Castles often had round or square towers at points along the walls. These towers were taller than the walls so archers could fire at enemies outside the castle. Towers were often built to stick out from the walls for the same reason.

MINECRAFT MANIA

If you build towers on your castle and you have a bow and arrows, you can fire on enemies outside the walls just like medieval archers did!

You can't build anything truly round in *Minecraft*, because almost everything is made from blocks. However, if you follow plans like this, you can build towers that look sort of round.

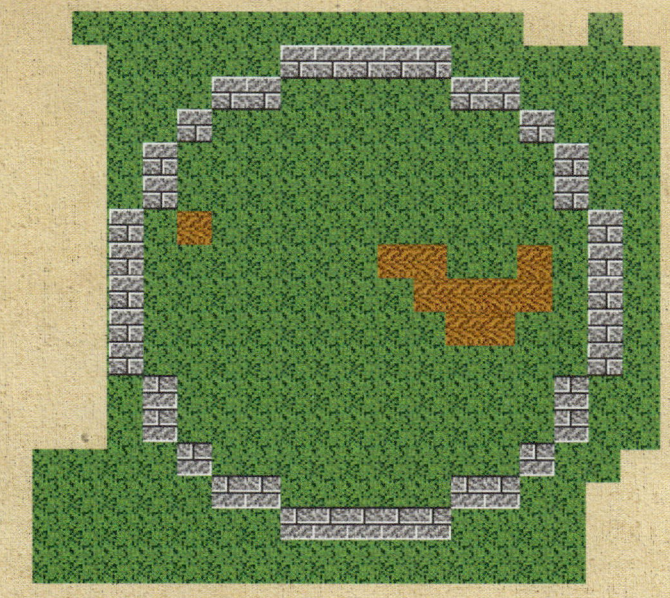

Inside the Walls

Inside your castle's walls, you can construct smaller buildings for storing supplies and stabling horses and other livestock. This is where they'd be kept in a real castle, too!

The keep should be the strongest part of the castle. In medieval times, it would contain living spaces, offices, more storage space, and a well. Enemies would have to go through all the castle's walls just to get to the keep, so this is where people would go to wait out a **siege**. You can put your bed and all your prized possessions in the keep.

You can decorate the inside of your keep however you'd like. You could use fancy blocks such as gold or diamonds. You could make a stained glass window!

Moats and Drawbridges

Many castles also have moats and drawbridges as further defenses. A moat is a deep, wide channel full of water running around the outside of a castle. A drawbridge is a bridge that can be lowered over a moat to let people in or raised to keep people out.

You can dig a moat outside your *Minecraft* castle and fill it with buckets of water, but it'll take a lot of work! You could also build your castle in the bend of a river and then just dig the moat the rest of the way around.

MINECRAFT MANIA

The physics of water in *Minecraft* works differently from the physics of water in real life. *Minecraft* water only spreads out so much. You may have to experiment to get your moat to work.

In *Minecraft*, you can easily build a drawbridge that's always down, but if you know how to use redstone, you can build a drawbridge or gate that opens and closes!

What Will You Build?

Castles were a major defense for people during medieval times. However, as time went on and people created guns and other more powerful weapons, these large strongholds became a thing of the past. Many castles still stand today and you can visit many of them.

Minecraft castles can protect you and your in-game possessions just like castles protected people in medieval times. And because of the possibilities of *Minecraft*, you can plan and build castles medieval people never dreamed of. You could make a floating castle or a castle made of diamond. The sky's the limit!

Even an army of zombies would have a hard time getting into this castle. Your hard-earned treasure is safe!

Making Mods

You can make your *Minecraft* creations even more exciting with modifications, or mods. Using a computer program called ScriptCraft, you can create new blocks, change the way the game functions, and make your own games. Imagine what you could build! How about a candy castle under a pink sky? Or a space-themed metal castle under the stars?

If you're interested in learning how to create mods in *Minecraft*, visit the website below. You'll find the information needed to get started with ScriptCraft and build your own *Minecraft* mods. **https://scriptcraftjs.org**

Glossary

biome: A natural community of plants and animals, such as a forest or desert.

concentric: Having a common center.

defense: A way of guarding against an enemy.

design: The pattern or shape of something. Also, to create the pattern or shape of something.

explosive: Something that causes an explosion, or a sudden release of energy.

fortify: To add material for strengthening or improving.

medieval: Having to do with the Middle Ages, a time in European history from about 500 to 1500.

mode: A form of something that is different from other forms of the same thing.

Normans: One of the Scandinavian conquerors of Normandy, France, in the 10th century.

physics: The study of matter, energy, force, motion, and the relationship among them; also the properties and composition of something.

resource: Something that can be used.

scaffolding: A system of scaffolds, or raised platforms for workers to sit or stand on.

siege: The operations of an army around a place for the purpose of forcing its occupants to give up.

Index

A
arches, 9

B
biome, 10
blast resistance, 13
blocks, 8, 15, 22

C
Cardiff Castle, 11
concentric castles, 12

D
drawbridges, 18, 19

E
Europe, 6

G
gravity, 8

K
keep, 12, 16, 17

M
moats, 18
modes, 8, 10, 14, 22
motte-and-bailey castles, 12

N
Neuschwanstein Castle, 6, 7
Normans, 6

P
physics, 8, 18

R
redstone, 19

S
ScriptCraft, 22
stone keep castles, 12

T
TNT, 10, 13
towers, 5, 12, 14, 15

V
villages, 10

W
walls, 6, 11, 12, 14, 16

Websites

Due to the changing nature of Internet links, PowerKids Press has developed an online list of websites related to the subject of this book. This site is updated regularly. Please use this link to access the list: www.powerkidslinks.com/stemmc/castles